D1525170

called
to this

Holiness and Love in 1 & 2 Peter

Lifeway Press®
Brentwood, Tennessee

ISBN 978-1-0877-7415-2
Item 005839488
Dewey Decimal Classification Number: 242
Subject Heading: DEVOTIONAL LITERATURE / BIBLE STUDY AND TEACHING / GOD

Printed in the United States of America.

Student Ministry Publishing
Lifeway Resources
200 Powell Place, Suite 100
Brentwood, TN 37027

We believe that the Bible has God for its author; salvation for its end; truth, without any mixture of error, for its matter; and that all Scripture is totally true and trustworthy. To review Lifeway's doctrinal guideline, please visit www.lifeway.com/doctrinalguideline.

publishing team

Director, Student Ministry
Ben Trueblood

Editorial Team Leader
Karen Daniel

Writer
Mary Margaret West

Content Editor
Kyle Wiltshire

Production Editor
April-Lyn Caouette

Graphic Designer
Shiloh Stufflebeam

Table of Contents

Intro

Peter was a fisherman turned preacher. Not your standard career path, right? Even though he was one of Jesus's best friends, he could be a bit unpredictable. When it came time to write letters to believers in his day, however, he was laser focused. He wrote with great authority and spoke with urgency. Peter's whole goal was to serve as an encouragement and a reminder to the people. Jesus was his great friend and hero, and Peter wanted to honor Jesus's life, death, and resurrection at every opportunity.

Peter was vital to the formation of the church as we know it today. Jesus entrusted a lot of responsibility to Peter, and Peter didn't miss a beat. Don't forget—this is the same man who denied Jesus three times on the night of His death! Peter wasn't perfect, but he had a clear life purpose. He didn't want to be remembered by his failures but by how he pointed people to Jesus.

Throughout these two letters, you'll see the obstacles that the believers of that day were facing. Peter's message to them was a challenge to step up with boldness and in humility. He didn't want anyone to hurt the name of Jesus. He wanted them to serve and love Him with everything they had.

There's much we can learn from Peter's life story. We'll spend the next thirty days learning from his experiences, reading the letters he wrote, and being challenged to live a life worthy of Jesus's sacrifice.

Getting Started

*This devotional contains thirty days of content, broken down into sections. Each day is divided into three elements—**discover**, **delight**, and **display**—to help you grow in your faith.*

discover

This section helps you examine the passage in light of who God is and determine what it says about your identity in relationship to Him. Included here is the daily Scripture reading and key verses, along with illustrations and commentary to guide you as you learn more about God's Word.

delight

In this section, you'll be challenged by questions and activities that help you see how God is alive and active in every detail of His Word and your life.

display

Here's where you take action. This section calls you to apply what you've learned through each day.

Each day also includes a prayer activity at the conclusion of the devotion.

Throughout the devotional, you'll also find extra items to help you connect with the topic personally, such as Scripture memory verses and interactive articles.

1 Peter

SECTION 1

No one thought Peter
was worthy of what
God called him to
do, but it didn't stop
him from preaching
anytime he had the
opportunity. He said
yes to Jesus's call
to leave his fishing
nets and follow Him,
and he never looked
back. His friendship
with Jesus allowed
him to have an
insider's perspective
on what our lives
should look like as we
follow Jesus.

Peter Who?

discover

READ 1 PETER 1:1-2.

Peter, an apostle of Jesus Christ . . .
— 1 Peter 1:1a

Peter was an uneducated fisherman and one of the least likely people to write books that would one day be included in the Bible. He was rough around the edges, had a fiery personality, and loved Jesus like a brother and best friend. His name was Simon, but Jesus changed it to Peter (Cephas) which means "rock." And he was one of the founders of the early church! That's quite a promotion from lowly, stinky fisherman.

Peter was a part of Jesus's inner circle. Since Peter, James, and John were the disciples to whom Jesus was the closest, Peter's perspective shows the close friendship they had during Jesus's three years of ministry on earth. Jesus called Peter to follow him, and Peter dropped everything to do just that. He was passionate about Jesus's life and ministry. However, he also struggled with doubt and fear. On the night of Jesus's death, Peter let his fear get hold of him so much that he denied even knowing his friend! He was afraid of what might happen if people associated him with Jesus. In a lot of ways, Peter was a hot mess. This reality makes it a lot easier for us to relate to him, and it helps us see that we aren't alone in our messiness.

These two letters were written to encourage believers, especially during hard times. Over the next thirty days, you'll hear Peter's own words exactly as he wrote them two thousand years ago. They're meant to encourage you right now. Don't miss out!

delight

In what areas of your life do you need encouragement right now?

What do you hope to get out of these next thirty days of learning from 1 & 2 Peter?

display

You're going to have a day when you don't want to get into God's Word, so prepare yourself now. What will you do when you don't want to make the time to grow? If you aren't reading this with a friend, find someone who will hold you accountable as you commit the next few weeks to walking through this devotional.

God, open my eyes to see and my heart to be changed by Your Word. Let me learn from You first and foremost, and let me be different as a result of what You've taught me. Amen.

Joy in Everything

discover

READ 1 PETER 1:3-9.

Though you have not seen him, you love him; though not seeing him now, you believe in him, and you rejoice with inexpressible and glorious joy, because you are receiving the goal of your faith, the salvation of your souls.
— 1 Peter 1:8-9

It's crazy to think that these letters were written nearly two thousand years ago. In spite of their age, they still have a ton of meaning for you today. The Bible stands the test of time, and we can learn from what Peter wrote way back then. In these verses, Peter was encouraging the people who were reading his letters: Christians who were facing persecution.

You've never seen Jesus with your own eyes, but you can still know Him personally, which is pretty awesome. Peter said that belief in Jesus isn't about what you see, but the joy you have in knowing Him. It's like when you're in a competition—the goal is to win, right? As Christians, the goal is knowing Jesus, which gives us joy that we can't explain in any other way than this: it's because we know Him.

Does this mean that everything is amazing and wonderful all the time? No way. It means that because you know Jesus, you have hope and joy in any circumstance you face. Life is still hard, but He is always good and is working in every situation. The reward these verses talk about is the same for you as for the people who saw Jesus with their own eyes. If you are saved, you get to spend eternity with Him in heaven! I can't think of a better reward than that.

delight

What is something you can't see but you know exists?

How does it feel to know that God has such a big plan for people who have a relationship with Him?

According to verse 9, what is the goal of your faith? Why is this so important to keep at the forefront of our minds?

display

Do the people around you know that you know Jesus? I hope so! It's not too late to make sure they do and to be really intentional about it. Your life should look different because of Jesus, and your friends and classmates should be able to see a difference. Think about one or two ways you can be intentional this week about making sure the people in your life know that you love Jesus.

If you're having trouble finding joy, ask God to help you experience joy in Him today. Pray that He would give you joy that doesn't even make sense, no matter what the situation. Ask God to let the people in your life see your joy on display so they can see Him in your life.

Called to This

What a Time to Be Alive

discover

READ 1 PETER 1:10-12.

It was revealed to them that they were not serving themselves but you. These things have now been announced to you through those who preached the gospel to you by the Holy Spirit sent from heaven — angels long to catch a glimpse of these things.
— 1 Peter 1:12

Believe it or not, there will be events in your lifetime that you'll one day read about in history books (and it will make you feel old). You'll talk to people younger than you who didn't experience these things firsthand. You'll try to explain to them, but you'll end up saying, "You had to be there to understand it. The pictures and videos just don't do it justice." In a similar way, Peter was trying to help believers of his day realize what a privilege it was to live during and after the time of Jesus.

Have you ever heard someone say, "What a time to be alive"? This is what Peter was essentially telling the people he was writing to. They had an incredible privilege to be alive in the time right after Jesus had fulfilled so much prophecy. There were prophets, teachers, believers, and even angels who had longed to be the ones to witness the life of Jesus with their own eyes. They had been anticipating the time that the Messiah would come and accomplish everything God had for Him to do.

Think about these people who were obedient to God, not knowing whether or not they would get to see the Messiah (that is, Jesus) for themselves. Verse 12 says that it "was revealed to them that they were not serving themselves but you." It's a reminder for you to stay the course and be faithful, even though you might be doing it for the benefit of those who will come after you.

delight

What is an event that you've experienced in your lifetime that you will one day want to tell your kids or grandkids about?

Why is it a privilege for us to live on this side of Jesus's life, death, and resurrection?

How do you feel about situations where you're not doing things for yourself but for the benefit of others?

display

There are people in countries around the world who can't talk openly about Jesus and where copies of the Bible are hard to come by. If you're reading this, you probably live in a place where you can talk about Jesus freely. Take a few minutes to pray for people who don't have easy access to the gospel of Jesus. Thank God that you can worship Him and live for Him without threat of opposition.

As you pray for people who can't easily share about Jesus, pray that God would give them the strength they need to stand up for Him, no matter what. Pray for opportunities for them to share the gospel of Jesus with others. Also pray that God would give you the chance to talk to people in your life about Him.

True Value

READ 1 PETER 1:13-21.

For you know that you were redeemed from your empty way of life inherited from your ancestors, not with perishable things like silver or gold, but with the precious blood of Christ, like that of an unblemished and spotless lamb.
— 1 Peter 1:18-19

Have you ever ruined something that had value to someone else? Yikes. That's not an easy thing to explain or own up to. Sometimes the things that matter the most don't have a lot of earthly value, but other times they do! What if your dog chewed up your new pair of shoes? You know, the ones that you don't want to get dirty and that are still perfectly white because you hardly wear them? What kind of value have you placed on things that are only temporary?

Peter was trying to show his readers that their lives were bought with the blood of Jesus, which is priceless. It can't be bought or sold on eBay, and it's more precious than any belonging we could have. You have to choose to live in a way where you are choosing Jesus daily. You're choosing to be holy because He is holy. Peter's words encourage us to throw off old ways of living and to live completely for Jesus. Jesus gave His life for us so that we can be redeemed, forgiven, and given new life.

Does this mean we can't own amazing shoes? Nope. What it means is that we must treasure Jesus more than those shoes or anything else this world has to offer. Without a relationship with Jesus, we have no hope of eternal life.

delight

What does it mean to be "redeemed"?

What are things you're tempted to value more than knowing Jesus?

How can you make sure to put Jesus first in all areas of your life?

display

Treasuring and valuing Jesus is a lifelong journey. It's so easy to be caught up in the things we can see, touch, taste, and feel that are right in front of us. We have to constantly keep Jesus as the focus of our lives, but that's not always easy. When the truth sinks in—that Jesus gave His life for us so that we can be redeemed, forgiven, and given new life—it changes everything. It begins to be the thing that shapes us and gives us direction.

Today, pray that God would help you keep Jesus in focus all day long. Pray for opportunities to share what you believe with the people God has put in your life. Ask God to help you become holy because He is holy.

Called to This

MEMORY VERSE
1 Peter 1:8-9

Though you have not
seen him,
you love him;
though not seeing him now,
you believe in him,
and you rejoice with
inexpressible and
glorious joy,
because you are receiving
the goal of your faith,
the salvation
of your souls.

Enduring Forever

discover

READ 1 PETER 1:22-25.

For "All flesh is like grass, and all its glory like a flower of the grass. The grass withers, and the flower falls, but the word of the Lord endures forever." And this word is the gospel that was proclaimed to you.
— 1 Peter 1:24-25

It's hard to imagine something that never fades, withers, or goes away. So much of what we have and own is breakable, fragile, and temporary. It's been said that a pack of Twinkies will last forever, but there's probably a point at which even the biggest daredevil wouldn't eat them. We're aware that life is fleeting and won't last forever. So it's amazing to think that "the word of the Lord endures forever" (v. 25).

The other part you don't want to miss from these verses is where it says, "For all flesh is like grass, and all its glory like a flower of the grass" (v. 24). All the glory we achieve here on earth doesn't last. That's a hard pill to swallow. All the things we work for (except for the things of Jesus) are temporary and fleeting. All our awards, praises, prizes, collections, or valuables aren't going to stand the test of time like Jesus will.

God's Word is the only thing that will last. As a Christian, this is the idea we build our lives upon. It's a huge deal. This is why it's important to spend time with Him (like you're doing today), and this is why it's the lens that we need to look through as we make decisions. The life, death, and resurrection of Jesus are enough for us to stake our lives on Him.

Why is it so easy to trust in things that don't last?

On the flip side, why can it be hard to trust in Jesus even when we know He can be trusted?

What does it mean in verse 25 when it says that "the word of the Lord endures forever"?

display

What's one thing you can do differently over the next week to let your life show that Jesus is more important than the temporary things you're surrounded by? Ask God to show you how to keep your eyes fixed on Him, even when it gets hard.

God, I need You to help me trust in You, even when the world wants all of my attention. Help me identify the things that are temporary and put my focus on the things that are of You. Let my life be a reflection of who You are to the world. Amen.

Get Rid of the Junk

READ 1 PETER 2:1-6.

**Therefore, rid yourselves of all malice, all deceit,
hypocrisy, envy, and all slander.
— 1 Peter 2:1**

Today's key verse is one that we can imagine a white-haired professor reading out loud—it uses a lot of big fancy words. Let's try to break it down and see what those words actually mean. But before we do that, pause and answer the first question on the next page to see if you can figure out what this verse is talking about.

When you boil it down, Peter is talking about getting rid of anything mean, hateful, untrue, hypocritical, jealous, and false in your life. Easy, right? He's telling us to get rid of the junk in our lives so we can live for Jesus and Jesus alone. The more we get to know God through His Word, the more we will do this. If you just try to make a bunch of changes so you can say you've done it, you won't get very far. It's when God's Word becomes the thing you live by that your life begins to change in a sustainable way. You begin to make changes out of your love for God, not just because you're supposed to.

God's Word isn't just for the people to whom it was written thousands of years ago. It's for us to learn from today. If you get lost or confused, ask for help! Don't try to go at it alone. Instead, find some adults who can help you as you learn.

delight

What do the terms "malice," "deceit," "hypocrisy," "envy," and "slander" found in verse 1 mean? (Feel free to use a dictionary, but don't get distracted on your phone!)

Is there something in your life that needs to change based on your understanding of the words in this verse?

What would it look like for you to truly love God's Word? How would the people in your life know that something is different?

display

One thing you can do is to actually pull out a physical Bible (if you have one) and read it. Underline, highlight, write notes, ask questions, and dig into it. So often, we get distracted when our only way of reading is on a phone or tablet. Ask God to give you a love for His Word like you've never had before in your relationship with Him.

As you pray today, ask God to show you time you can spend in His Word every day. Ask Him to give you a new love for it and to give you an understanding and a teachable spirit as you read. Trust God with the process and see how you grow!

Who Are You?

discover

READ 1 PETER 2:7-10.

But you are a chosen race, a royal priesthood, a holy nation, a people for his possession, so that you may proclaim the praises of the one who called you out of darkness into his marvelous light.
— 1 Peter 2:9

If you're on social media, what does your profile say about who you are? How do you identify yourself so that others know who you are? Maybe your profile mentions the year you'll graduate high school, where you live, or what sports and activities you're involved in. Those things help identify who you are, but those things are not who you are.

In today's passage, Peter reveals who you are. No matter what you've done, what others have said about you, or how you feel about yourself, these things are true about you—it's what you're called to be a part of because of Jesus. Are you living like it? As Christians, God has chosen you for His good purposes so that you can bring Him praise. There's no greater identity than that, but we easily forget what He says about us.

Culture is fighting to define who you are. It's like everyone wants to put a name tag on you, saying who you are. Are you going to let them do that, or are you going to let God define who you are and stand firm in it? Identifying with Jesus comes with power and authority, but it doesn't mean everyone around you will agree. You may face hatred or confusion from others because you identify with Jesus, but you'll never be alone. We are God's people, called into marvelous light, to give Him praise. When we identify with Him, we are cheered on by countless other believers.

delight

List 3–4 positive words you would use to describe yourself—who you truly are. Who in your life says these same things about you?

Are you living like these things that Peter and others say about you are true? Why or why not?

What is the goal of us living like we are who Peter says we are?

display

How can you cheer on other believers in their identity in Jesus? If you've ever felt lonely because you were outnumbered by people who don't believe what you believe, what would have encouraged you? Whom can you encourage this week to stand firm in Jesus? You are chosen and loved by God, and so are the other believers around you. Maybe it's someone you don't know very well but who you feel called to encourage. Do it! Don't miss the opportunity to really cheer someone else on.

God, show me who I can encourage this week. Help me to stand firm with You, no matter what. Remind me of who You say I am, especially when it gets hard. Let my life be an example to others around me so they can see You. Amen.

Toxic Cleanup

discover

READ 1 PETER 2:11-17.

Conduct yourselves honorably among the Gentiles, so that when they slander you as evildoers, they will observe your good works and will glorify God on the day he visits.
— 1 Peter 2:12

Standing up for Jesus can be hard. As believers, our lives should be lived in such a way that even those who oppose our faith would be unable to speak badly about us. Some people go about standing up for their faith in a way that offends other people, stirs up unnecessary conflict, and can honestly just be offensive. When we look at the Bible, Jesus spoke kindly and directly to those whom He was trying to speak truth.

Peter encouraged the believers of his day to honor the people and authorities around them because, in doing that, it would honor God. If you've ever spent much time around someone who was constantly complaining about other people and talking down to them, you know that behavior usually spreads quickly. A conversation can turn toxic in a hurry if you're not careful. The same is true for words that honor: they spread quickly.

Whether you're speaking to a teacher, a classmate, an influential leader, or a friend, kind words go a long way. It's not about saying things that are untrue; rather, it's about showing honor to people whom God created and whom He loves.

delight

Look at verse 17. What does it mean in practice to "Honor everyone. Love the brothers and sisters. Fear God. Honor the emperor"?

What are three ways you can do good to others around you?

display

You have an awesome opportunity to leverage your influence when it comes to honor. What if you were able to create a culture of honor wherever you go by the way you treat the people around you? It could really change things at home, at school, at church, at practice, or wherever you go during the week. If you find yourself in the middle of a toxic mess, be the one who helps clean it up by honoring the people around you well.

Pray that God would give you the words to honor and encourage the people you encounter today. Ask Him to show you ways you can honor those around you, even when it's hard.

Called to This

Be the Thermostat

discover

READ 1 PETER 2:18-25.

He did not commit sin, and no deceit was found in his mouth; when he was insulted, he did not insult in return; when he suffered, he did not threaten but entrusted himself to the one who judges justly.
— 1 Peter 2:22-23

Conflict is never fun to deal with. But Jesus gave us a powerful example of how to deal with conflict, and Peter gave the believers of his day a reminder of what that looked like. Jesus set the example of how we are to live and our attitude and actions toward others. He did not match insult for insult. Instead, He humbled Himself and trusted God for the outcome. Easy, right? I wish it were.

It feels so much easier to either run and hide or to put on your boxing gloves and jump into the ring. Being humble like Jesus is the hardest response. Jesus wasn't a doormat who let people step all over Him, and He also didn't just react to what was going on around Him. He was like a thermostat: He set the temperature for what happened around Him. He wasn't like a thermometer, which simply reacts to what's happening. He stood strong in the midst of trials and loved the people around Him. Jesus was able to hold His head high, and that's what He wants us to do as well.

You aren't ever going to be perfect, but Jesus set an example of how He wants you to live. Humility usually brings surprising responses from the people around you because it's not what anyone expects. It's one of the ways that Jesus was so different from other leaders, and it's why He won the respect of those around Him, even those who disagreed.

delight

How would your friends and family say you handle conflicts that come up in your life?

What example did Jesus set for you in today's Scripture reading?

Living with humility can be difficult, but what's one way you can start being more humble in your daily life?

display

How can you be the thermostat in the situations you face so that you're leading humbly like Jesus? Whether your history is to react or run, think about ways you can set the tone wherever you go. Jesus was a quiet force for good, and you can be too.

Pray that God would give you wisdom in how you handle conflict when it comes up. Ask Him for direction and guidance as you speak and act so that your response is one of humility.

True Beauty

READ 1 PETER 3:1-7.

Don't let your beauty consist of outward things like elaborate hairstyles and wearing gold jewelry or fine clothes, but rather what is inside the heart — the imperishable quality of a gentle and quiet spirit, which is of great worth in God's sight.
— 1 Peter 3:3-4

We aren't going to skip over this passage just because it's talking about marriage. How you handle relationships now sets you up for the future. It's never too early to start to build a foundation for healthy relationships. Today's verses reveal that both husbands and wives should love, honor, and respect each other, but these teachings also carry over to every other relationship you're in.

These verses also reveal that true beauty comes from what is within, not from your appearance. If you've been on social media lately, you've probably realized that the world tells you the exact opposite. But God made you to be unique, and He does everything on purpose and with great intent. As much as it would be awesome to think your life will change if you change your style or buy those new sneakers everyone's talking about, it won't. True beauty is about your heart. It is revealed in how you show love, honor, and respect to those around you. Your true character is evident when you're the same person no matter who you're with.

The more comfortable you are with who God has created you to be, the healthier your relationships will likely be. The last part of today's key verse talks about having a "gentle and quiet spirit." This doesn't mean you're not allowed to talk. It means that your words are flooded with kindness and that you think before you speak. This is easy for some people but not for everyone. Regardless, it is a habit we all should practice.

delight

What qualities does the passage say are important to God?

What does your "beauty consist of"? (See v. 3.)

Would your friends and family say that your words are gentle and kind? Why or why not?

display

It's so much easier said than done to change your thinking about what true beauty really is. What if you started today? How much different would you feel in a week or a month? Heart change happens over time, and today is a great day to start thinking and talking about yourself differently—as God sees you, not as the world defines you.

God, help me to see myself the way You see me. Don't let me be distracted by the things the world offers, but let my heart reflect who You are every day. Amen.

The Upside Down

discover

READ 1 PETER 3:8-12.

Finally, all of you be like-minded and sympathetic, love one another, and be compassionate and humble, not paying back evil for evil or insult for insult but, on the contrary, giving a blessing, since you were called for this, so that you may inherit a blessing.
— 1 Peter 3:8-9

"They started it!" Have you ever said those words before? We often say this when we don't want to take responsibility for how we reacted to someone else's words or actions. Even if it wasn't our fault, we didn't start it, and it wasn't our idea, paying back evil for evil is definitely not how God wants us to handle difficult circumstances that come our way. He desires us to live life upside down, different than the world.

It takes a lot of courage to be humble and take ownership for our actions. It's much easier to play the blame game and push it off on someone else. This passage is a great example of how we're supposed to act opposite to how the world acts. We're supposed to show kindness, even when it's hard. This doesn't mean we're supposed to be doormats. It means that we need to stand up for the right things, without reacting in ungodly ways. It's usually so much easier to fly off the handle, rather than take the time to think before we respond.

Our culture tries to push the idea that we all get what we deserve. When we take the high road, we're being obedient to God. He's ultimately the One who judges and gives out consequences, not you. The world may tell us that "what goes around comes around," but God's grace and mercy are much greater than this.

delight

What do you think it means to be "like minded" as it states in verse 8?

Think of a time when you repaid evil for evil. What would you do differently if you could live that situation again today?

Called to This

display

If you start living like Peter encourages us to live, other people will notice. Pray that God would give you an opportunity this week to look like Jesus as you respond to the situations that come your way. Ask a friend or mentor to hold you accountable to living a different kind of life.

God, show me how to live like Jesus. Give me the courage to stand up for what I know is right and to show kindness to everyone I encounter this week, even the ones who are hard to love. Amen.

Are You Ready?

discover

READ 1 PETER 3:13-17.

But in your hearts regard Christ the Lord as holy, ready at any time to give a defense to anyone who asks you for a reason for the hope that is in you. Yet do this with gentleness and reverence, keeping a clear conscience, so that when you are accused, those who disparage your good conduct in Christ will be put to shame.
— 1 Peter 3:15-16

When you have the opportunity to share the gospel, don't act surprised! If you ask God to give you the chance, He probably will. Our mission here on earth is to share the gospel with the people God puts in our life. Peter challenged us to be "ready at any time to give a defense to anyone who asks you for a reason for the hope that is in you" (1 Pet. 3:15). Are you ready?

If you don't know how to share how Jesus has changed your life, talk to a youth pastor, a parent or guardian, or another godly adult in your life and ask him or her to help you. It's as simple as sharing your own story of how you came to know Jesus. Peter reminded us that people will still criticize and accuse us of doing wrong, so we have to be gentle and kind in our response. (See Day 11 for a refresher on how to do this.) It's hard to be gentle and kind when someone is accusing you!

Remember, few people are argued, shouted at, and shamed into accepting Jesus. We must present the good news with kindness and respect. Not all the people with whom you share will choose to put their faith in Jesus, but seek to take the opportunities that God gives you.

delight

Do you feel ready to share the gospel with someone in your life? Why or why not?

How can you live as an example to the world around you so people will wonder what's different about you?

display

It's time to be ready if you aren't yet. You may have shared your Jesus story before, but maybe you haven't. Consider practicing with a friend so you feel comfortable, and pray that God will give you courage and wisdom. Use the space below to write out how you came to know Christ as your Savior. Use three elements:

Life before knowing Jesus:

How you came to know Jesus:

Life since placing your faith in Him:

Pray for opportunities to share the gospel in your circle of influence. Ask God to make you bold like Peter and to always be ready to share.

Called to This

MEMORY VERSE

1 Peter 2:9

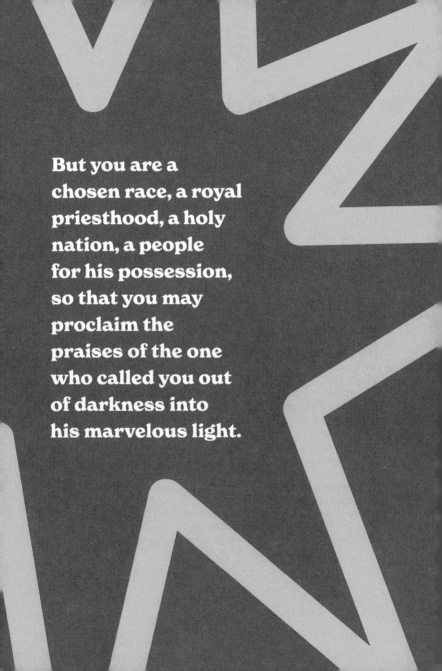

But you are a chosen race, a royal priesthood, a holy nation, a people for his possession, so that you may proclaim the praises of the one who called you out of darkness into his marvelous light.

Made Alive

discover

READ 1 PETER 3:18-22.

**For Christ also suffered for sins once for all, the righteous
for the unrighteous, that he might bring you to God. He was
put to death in the flesh but made alive by the Spirit.
— 1 Peter 3:18**

Jesus changes everything. Peter explains that when you put your faith in Jesus, it is the Spirit who makes us alive in Christ. Jesus's sacrifice on the cross made a way for us to know God personally, and our lives should show it every day. He died for all people. None of us are saved as a result of our own goodness.

It's kind of like Noah. Remember him from the Old Testament? He's the guy that God told to build a giant boat because a flood was coming. Noah stood up and did exactly what God told him to do, and it made all the difference in the world. Noah is a picture of Jesus. Noah's family was saved on the Ark because of his righteousness. We are saved by the righteousness of Jesus, not our own.

Have you been made alive in Christ? If you haven't, today is a great time to ask Jesus to become the Lord and Savior of your life. You can do that right now by praying, asking Him to forgive your sins and change your life. If you believe in Him and prayed that today, talk to an adult in your life who loves Jesus and who can walk you through some next steps.

delight

What is something about the Bible that you've struggled to believe because you couldn't see it?

How does your life show that you've been made alive by Jesus?

display

There's nothing like knowing Jesus and walking with Him. He did what we couldn't do so that we can live a life we don't deserve to live and spend eternity with Him in heaven. Does your life show that this is true? Can the people you're around tell that you know Jesus and that you live differently because of your relationship with Him? What needs to change? Re-read 1 Peter 3:22. If all of those things are subject to Jesus, what in your life needs to be subjected to Him?

God, let my life show that Jesus is my Lord and Savior. Help me to put Him first and to set an example for the other people I'm around. Thank You for saving me through Jesus! Amen.

Set Apart

discover

READ 1 PETER 4:1-6.

**They are surprised that you don't join them in the same
flood of wild living — and they slander you.
— 1 Peter 4:4**

If you read today's verses fast, go back and read them again. Peter again reinforced that our lives need to look different because of Jesus. We're supposed to be set apart, living differently than the world. Living this way may mean that some people won't want to be friends with you, but Jesus is worth it.

Has someone ever given you a hard time when you wouldn't do something because of your faith? Maybe you gave in and did something you regretted in order to fit in. We've all been there! Rather than living in shame over the past, let's look to Jesus and see what we can do differently from here on out.

There's so much peace and freedom in living in obedience to Jesus. While the temptation may be to do the thing to fit in, the feeling that gives you is temporary. Peace with Jesus is different. Whether it's what you post on social media, what you text about someone else, or the conversations that take place in the locker room, it all matters. What do those things say about who you truly are?

Are you willing to let others talk about you behind your back because you did the right thing? Life with Jesus isn't easy, but friend, it's SO worth it. You'll never regret choosing Jesus over the world. Others are looking to see if you're going to be consistent. They want to know if what you say and do are going to line up time and time again. Show them that Jesus makes all the difference in the world and that you're different because of Him.

delight

Knowing that Jesus sees how you spend your time, what should you do differently?

What kinds of "wild living" (v. 4) happens around you?

How can you honor God in a world that is wild?

display

Living a set-apart life demands consistency and faithfulness. When you don't feel like doing the right thing, pause right where you are and tell Jesus. He knows what it's like to be tempted and to choose to do the right thing anyway. He's familiar with everything you'll ever walk through, and He will be with you no matter what.

God, help me to trust You when it's hard. Help me to focus more on living a life that honors You than pleasing my friends. Keep me focused on You every day. Amen.

Called to This

Ready, Set, Go!

discover

READ 1 PETER 4:7-11.

**The end of all things is near; therefore, be alert
and sober-minded for prayer.
— 1 Peter 4:7**

What have you been gifted to do? Maybe you're an awesome basketball player, an incredible artist, or a theatrical standout. Those things are great, but what spiritual gifts do you have? What are the things that God has uniquely gifted you to do so that you can contribute to the kingdom? Those gifts are being called into action. Don't ignore the call. Time is running out.

Peter wrote this nearly two thousand years ago, and the end still hasn't come. Does that mean anything has changed? No! We should still be sober minded and live as if Jesus is returning today. Everything Peter wrote in this letter is building on itself. He wrote with great passion and urgency, and we need to read it that way. If he was passionate about it that long ago, we should be even more passionate today!

Throughout all of Peter's first letter, he wove together the theme of how followers of Jesus need to be ready. We have to love one another and live out the faith that Jesus set before us. The gifts that believers have been given through the Holy Spirit need to be used to bring honor and glory to God on a daily basis. If you don't know what your spiritual gifts are, search online for a "spiritual gifts" test and take one! You may be surprised at the results you find and how you can use your gifts now.

delight

Your spiritual gifts could be things like encouragement, teaching, administration, service, generosity, or leadership. Read Romans 12:6-8 and Ephesians 4:11-12. Which gifts do you think the Spirit may have given you?

Are you living ready for Jesus's return? What do you think needs to change so that you are ready?

display

Use your spiritual gifts this week. Don't let them go to waste! Ask God for an opportunity to put them into practice, even in a new or different way.

Pray that God would be honored through your gifts. Ask Him to prepare your heart to always be ready and prepared for His return and live with the end in mind.

Detention

discover

READ 1 PETER 4:12-19.

Dear friends, don't be surprised when the fiery ordeal comes among you to test you, as if something unusual were happening to you.
— 1 Peter 4:12

If one of your friends has had detention after school, have you ever offered to go in their place? No way! You weren't the one who caused the problem. Why should you have to go through the misery of sitting in detention? Well, following Jesus means that sometimes we might have to sit in what feels like detention, even when we don't deserve it. He never said following Him would be easy, but He says over and over that it's worth it.

Peter made the point that we may not have signed up for suffering, but it's a part of walking with Jesus. We often act so surprised when suffering comes as a result of knowing Jesus, but it shouldn't be a shock. In 1 Peter 4:13, Peter says to "rejoice as you share in the sufferings of Christ, so that you may also rejoice with great joy when his glory is revealed." Rejoicing and suffering feel like complete opposites, but Peter said we are to merge the two together and rejoice when we suffer. When we do this, we identify with Jesus Himself.

Blessings are the result when we face these trials and endure through them. God is with us every step of the way, and He is never caught off guard by anything. Going through ridicule and being mocked by people when you stand up for Jesus will come back as blessings. It all feels so backwards, but Jesus said this is the way. Your job is to keep your eyes fixed on Him.

delight

What do you think it means to "share in the sufferings of Christ"?

How have you seen someone suffer for Jesus? What has been the result of their suffering?

display

When you're called to stand up for Jesus, you'll never be alone. God promises His presence no matter what, and when you face suffering, you join with countless other believers over the centuries who have stood strong in their faith. Keep your eyes fixed on Jesus. Take a moment and pray the prayer below. Ask God to prepare your heart not if but when hardship comes your way.

When it gets hard, God, give me the courage to be brave and bold for Your name. Help me to hold my head up high so that You can be honored through my life. Amen.

Called to This

Old People

discover

READ 1 PETER 5:1-5.

**In the same way, you who are younger, be subject
to the elders. All of you clothe yourselves with
humility toward one another, because God resists
the proud but gives grace to the humble.
— 1 Peter 5:5**

Most likely, you're not considered an "elder" if you're reading this devotional. You're probably a teenager, and it'll be a long time before you can take on a title like this. Sometimes an elder just refers to someone who is older than us, but in this passage, the elders are those who have been given authority to lead God's people and shepherd them. In the local church, they are often also called pastors.

So what does this mean for you? You're supposed to listen to the elders, and they're supposed to lead you in a way that is obedient to Jesus. Having respect for our elders—both those who are leaders in the church and those who are simply older than us—is so important. We are to give them respect, even if we don't feel like they deserve it. These elders are held accountable by God for the way they live their lives and how they lead the people God has entrusted to them. It's a huge weight of responsibility that they carry, and something they should take seriously.

This passage also talks about how God wants us to be humble, not prideful. Walking humbly is the path to experiencing true grace. It's not always easy, but what is? God's desire is that we would show humility to those around us. That's how we become grace-filled. At the end of the day, our lives should show that we know Jesus, and we should be able to point out the people in our lives who have modeled it well.

Are there any "elders" in your life who you can learn from? If so, who?

How can you practically show humility to the people in your life?

Why is it sometimes hard to respect our elders? What does God call us to do?

display

Sometimes we want to think of our elders as old people who don't know what they're talking about. What if we turned the tables and thought of them as wise people who have had a lot of life experience? What if you took the opportunity to reach out to them and ask some questions about God? Don't miss out! Seek out an opportunity to connect with an older person in your life who loves Jesus and to draw from their deep wells of experience.

Today, take a few minutes to pray for the elders and pastors who you know. Pray that God would use them to set an example for you and the other people they serve. Ask God to give them hearts that represent Him well.

Never Alone

READ 1 PETER 5:6-9.

**Resist him, firm in the faith, knowing that the
same kind of sufferings are being experienced by
your fellow believers throughout the world.
— 1 Peter 5:9**

You're not alone. The feelings, emotions, experiences, and trials you face happen to teenagers all over the world. The same enemy that does everything he can do to throw you off track is doing the same thing to them as well. These things have been happening for the past two thousand years.

If you're walking with Jesus, the devil hates it and wants to stop you. When you spend time with God, He gives you wisdom and insight from the Bible that will help you be ready for whatever attacks come your way. Here are a few truths from these verses you don't want to miss:

- God is the one who will exalt you if you're humble (v. 6).

- We can give all of our cares and problems to God—He wants them (v. 7)!

- Believers have to be ready to face the devil's attacks (v. 8).

- The devil can be resisted because other believers around the world are experiencing the same things (v. 9).

- You are never alone. Jesus is always with you (see Matt. 28:20).

Called to This

delight

How does it feel to know that other believers around the world are facing the same trials that you are?

What are some problems and cares you need to give to God so that He can carry them for you?

What can you do to remind yourself that you are never alone?

display

As a believer, you've been given so much power to live out your faith boldly. When things get hard, be reminded and encouraged that others have walked and are walking through difficulties just like yours. And even when it feels like you're alone, Jesus is always with you. Write the words "Not Alone" on a sticky note. Place this note somewhere you will see it often to remind yourself that Jesus is with you.

Pray for other believers around the world who are facing trials. Ask God to protect them, give them hope, and help them to stand firm in their faith.

Rest in Truth

discover

READ 1 PETER 5:10-14.

The God of all grace, who called you to his eternal glory in Christ, will himself restore, establish, strengthen, and support you after you have suffered a little while.
— 1 Peter 5:10

We're at the end of 1 Peter! Peter wrapped up this letter with a word of encouragement to the believers of his day. He wrote, "The God of all grace, who called you to his eternal glory in Christ, will himself restore, establish, strengthen, and support you after you have suffered a little while" (1 Pet. 5:10). Whew. God is the One who cares for us when we suffer. Aren't you thankful for that? He has chosen you to be a part of His family, and He has promised to care for you.

God will give you everything you need in order to do what He has called you to do, even when it's hard. All the power and authority belong to God, and you must constantly point it back to Him. None of us have what it takes to live God-honoring lives on our own. We can only do it in His strength.

If we suffer for Jesus, we can rest in the truth that it will be only for a while and that Jesus has our backs. He will restore, strengthen, establish, and support us. He's in charge, and He knows everything. Nothing catches Him by surprise. He cares for us and loves us more than we can imagine, and Peter made sure all who heard or read his letter knew this.

delight

How have you seen Jesus restore, strengthen, establish, and support you?

How can you encourage other believers when they have a hard time trusting God?

display

Suffering is bound to happen. What would it look like if you chose to be joyful when you experienced suffering because you knew that God was at work? Just like many other things we've learned in this letter, this may feel upside down, but God works the best doing things only He can do. Take a few moments and carefully pray using the prompt below. Don't rush. Focus on what God might want to say to you during this time.

Pray today that when you suffer, you can choose joy. Ask God to give you strength that can only come from Him so that you can stand steadfast in truth.

2 Peter

SECTION 2

As Peter's life drew to a close, he had one last opportunity to speak to the believers and the churches that he loved so much. He held nothing back, and He expected everyone to follow his example and live passionately for Jesus all of their days as well.

Inside-Out Process

discover

READ 2 PETER 1:1-11.

For this very reason, make every effort to supplement your faith with goodness, goodness with knowledge, knowledge with self-control, self-control with endurance, endurance with godliness, godliness with brotherly affection, and brotherly affection with love.
— 2 Peter 1:5-7

Did you know that God has given you everything you need to live a life that honors Him? Because of the Holy Spirit, you have what it takes right inside of you! It's amazing to think about. When you came to know Jesus personally, so many changes happened that you couldn't even see. Growing in faith truly is an inside-out process, and there's room for growth throughout your whole life. If you ever talk to someone who seems like they know everything, don't worry: they don't!

If you've ever read about the "fruit of the Spirit" (see Gal. 5), the words that Peter uses here should be familiar. He's reminding believers that God has given us promises that we know He will fulfill and that the gifts He has given are to keep us out of trouble. When we use these gifts every day, it helps us grow in our faith and stand strong when things get tough.

If all of this is new to you, don't stress! Growing in the Lord is a process, and it takes daily intentionality. You're on the right track, so don't give up! The gifts that Peter says we're given are for all of us. Goodness, knowledge, self-control, endurance, godliness, brotherly and sisterly affection, and love are all qualities that you have been given if you know Jesus. Does it feel like those things are a part of your life?

delight

To whom is Peter writing this letter? (See 2 Pet. 1:1.)

Of the gifts that Peter listed (or out of the fruit of the Spirit from Galatians 5), in which areas do you need to grow the most?

display

It sounds great to think of all the fruit of the Spirit that is available to you, but which area do you need to put into practice most this week? Choose one that you feel like you can use intentionally, and see what happens!

Pray that God would show you ways to grow in the fruit of the Spirit. Ask Him to give you opportunities to exercise this evidence of the work of the Spirit in your life.

Wake Up

discover

READ 2 PETER 1:12-15.

**I think it is right, as long as I am in this bodily tent,
to wake you up with a reminder.
— 2 Peter 1:13**

What in the world is a "bodily tent"? Peter was referring to his earthly body as a tent—a temporary home. We can tell that Peter was older when he wrote this because he referenced how he might not be alive much longer and would "soon lay aside my tent" (2 Pet. 1:14). Who is that older believer that helps "wake you up" when you need it?

Are you a morning person, or do you hit the snooze button as many times as you can while still having just enough time to get out the door? Waking up is hard to do! Peter wrote that he wanted to wake the people up with a reminder of the truths they already knew. Do you ever need a reminder of something you already know? Whether it's a note you put in your phone, writing something on your hand, or literally telling someone to remind you, we need reminders of all kinds. We can't remember everything.

Peter wouldn't always be around to remind them, so he wrote these things down so his fellow believers would always have them. His letters still serve as a hopeful and helpful reminder to us of how God wants us to live. Peter loved these believers and didn't want them to miss out on God's best for them. What a blessing that we have his letter today to give us the same reminders when we feel lost or hopeless.

Called to This

delight

If you knew you were old and nearing the end of your life, what would you say to the people who are important to you?

What's something you need to be reminded of often when it comes to God's promises?

display

Think of someone who is important to you. Write them a text or a handwritten note this week and tell this person how much she or he means to you! Remind this person of what he or she has done to impact your life.

God, help me to remember what Your Word says about who I am. Let me be a reminder of Your goodness and faithfulness to the people You've put in my life. Let my life be full of the truth. Amen.

Eye Witness

discover

READ 2 PETER 1:16-21.

**For we did not follow cleverly contrived myths when we made
known to you the power and coming of our Lord Jesus Christ;
instead, we were eyewitnesses of his majesty.
— 2 Peter 1:16**

It's always easier to believe something if you've seen it with your own eyes. Peter reminded the believers that he had seen Jesus with his own eyes; he wasn't making up something mystical or mysterious. Jesus is the real deal. Peter had walked and talked with Him. He and the other disciples had been eyewitnesses to the life, death, and resurrection of Jesus. They knew, better than anyone, that what Jesus taught, spoke, and lived was real and worthy of giving our lives to.

The prophecies that were spoken by people and recorded in Scripture were always from God, not from the people themselves. God has the power and authority to speak through His people. Now it was Peter's turn to be one of the people speaking for God. He was obedient to proclaim God's message. As a result, he was effective to tell countless people about Jesus through preaching in the churches that he helped establish. He wrote that he and his fellow apostles "were eyewitnesses of [Jesus's] majesty" (2 Pet. 1:16). Can you imagine? What a privilege to be there and see it all firsthand!

We still get to see God's majesty on display today; it just looks different for us. One day, those of us who have put our faith in Him will see His majesty face to face. What an amazing sight that will be! For now, we must put our trust in the words of God that were recorded by faithful witnesses like Peter.

delight

Is it hard for you to believe in Jesus since you haven't seen Him in the flesh? Why or why not?

If you could ask Peter a question about what it was like to walk with Jesus as his friend, what would you ask? Why?

display

Take a couple of minutes and make a list of big events that you've seen with your own eyes. Examples could be significant family moments, other moments you've celebrated, or world events. How would you describe these events to someone who wasn't a witness to them? How did you see God shaping those moments?

Ask God to give you eyes to see Him clearly, even though you haven't seen Him with your own eyes. Thank Him for giving you the words of Scripture to learn from.

The Real Deal

discover

READ 2 PETER 2:1-3.

There were indeed false prophets among the people, just as there will be false teachers among you. They will bring in destructive heresies, even denying the Master who bought them, and will bring swift destruction on themselves.
— 2 Peter 2:1

Did you know that at Walt Disney World, adults aren't allowed to dress like the characters? This is because the employees don't want anyone to mistake visitors in costume for the real things. A grown man visiting Disney World? No problem! A grown man visiting Disney World dressed as Mickey Mouse? Sketch!

The older you get, the more you'll realize that there are false prophets all over the place. There are always people who come along and try to distort the Word of God—sometimes even people who claim to be Christians. We must have discernment and not chase after something just because it sounds good. We must instead lean on the truth.

How do you know who and what to believe? You have to know what the Bible says. Measure everything against God's Word. There's no other way to be able to see what's true and what's not!

According to Peter, the false teachers "will bring in destructive heresies, even denying the Master who bought them, and will bring swift destruction on themselves" (2 Pet. 2:1). While it feels like this would be so easy to spot, it isn't always! The enemy is crafty and smarter than we want to think he is, and he uses other people to deceive us. Be alert and ready!

delight

Have you ever mistaken someone or something for the real deal? How did you come to realize the truth of the situation?

What does 2 Peter 2:3 say will happen if we listen to false prophets?

display

Once you're done with this devotional, what are you going to read next? One way to stay in God's Word is to always have something to study. If you don't know yet, take some time today to figure it out!

God, help me to know Your Word so I can see what's true and what's false. Don't let me fall for the schemes of the enemy and people who want to distract me from You. Keep my eyes fixed on You. Amen.

Called to This

MEMORY VERSE

2 Peter 3:9

The Lord does not delay
his promise, as some
understand delay, but
is patient with you, not
wanting any to perish but
all to come to repentance.

Crime and Punishment

discover

READ 2 PETER 2:4-10a.

The Lord knows how to rescue the godly from trials and to keep the unrighteous under punishment for the day of judgment, especially those who follow the polluting desires of the flesh and despise authority.
— 2 Peter 2:9-10

God doesn't play: He does what He says He's going to do. We often hear about His kindness towards us, but we don't always talk about His justice. He is faithful to His Word, without fail. When God told us how He wanted us to act, He gave consequences that were harsh if we weren't obedient. God isn't out to get us; He's out to show that He's faithful and that He's serious about His Word.

It might be hard for some to imagine God like this, but it should make us grateful that He is willing to stand up for what He said He would do. This passage serves as a reminder that "the Lord knows how to rescue the godly from trials" and that this is for our benefit (see 2 Pet. 2:9). He always keeps His eyes on us, but we have to remember to keep our eyes fixed on Him. God doesn't move, and He tells us that He will rescue us from trials. It may not happen the way we want it to, but He keeps His Word.

The Lord knows how to watch after us. We can rest assured those who deny Him will be met with a terrible fate when they stand before Him. God has proven this over time; He provides for and cares for His children. It's up to us what we choose to do with His provision.

delight

Which Bible characters can you think of who suffered consequences because of their bad decisions?

How can you make sure that you live a righteous life before God?

display

Some people like to push the envelope and see if consequences really apply to them. Choose to live a life where you stick to the boundaries God has placed around you; these boundaries are for your own protection. How can you influence the people around you to do the same?

God, I want to keep my eyes fixed on You. Don't let me be distracted from the plans You have for me; help me stay close to You. Thank You for loving me even though I sometimes fail to do what You desire. Amen.

A Talking Donkey

discover

READ 2 PETER 2:10b-16.

They have gone astray by abandoning the straight path and have followed the path of Balaam, the son of Bosor, who loved the wages of wickedness but received a rebuke for his lawlessness: A speechless donkey spoke with a human voice and restrained the prophet's madness.
— 2 Peter 2:15-16

It feels like Peter went out into left field with this passage. It's kind of odd! He references the strange Old Testament story of Balaam. Balaam was a man who was paid to speak a word against God's people, but the Lord would not allow him to do so, no matter how many times he tried. God used Balaam's donkey to speak directly to him about what a mess he was making of the situation (see Num. 20). Can you picture it—a talking donkey?!

Have you ever talked about something you really didn't have any authority to talk about? Sometimes we do it to sound smart and authoritative, but we have to be really careful here, because this is what Peter said was leading to the destruction of people in his day. They were using false words to slander—that is, to damage the reputation of—other people.

This still happens today very visibly in situations like political elections, and it also happens at school and on social media on a daily basis. People can be really crafty with their words to do real damage to the reputation of others. Unfortunately, it doesn't take much to change people's minds. God is honored when we speak well of other people. We aren't supposed to lie but to instead speak the truth about the people we encounter and honor them well.

Called to This

delight

How have you seen negative words affect someone's reputation?

What is God calling you to do when it comes to speaking honestly about the people in your life?

display

If speaking honestly about others (either to their faces or behind their backs) doesn't come naturally to you, now is a great time to begin to change things. Ask a friend or mentor to hold you accountable to only speak the truth about others, and see what God can do!

God, let my words be honoring of the people in my life. You love them all and created them in Your image. Help me to reflect You in everything I say and do. Amen.

Snowball Effect

discover

READ 2 PETER 2:17-22.

They promise them freedom, but they themselves are slaves of corruption, since people are enslaved to whatever defeats them.
— 2 Peter 2:19

Have you ever heard of the snowball effect? It's the idea that something can start small but grow bigger and bigger over time. The classic example is a snowball rolling downhill, picking up more and more snow until it's huge. In reality, snow doesn't always act like this, but sin does. Sin can look promising, but it's only a path to destruction and corruption. Anyone who tries to convince you otherwise is a liar who is leading you astray. Small actions or little white lies may start innocent, but like that snowball, their negative effects will only grow and grow.

Peter recognized that some of the people he was writing to were deep into sin yet had once called themselves followers of Jesus. It was hard for him to wrap his mind around the fact that they knew the truth but had walked away from it, as if they had never heard it in the first place.

Sin may look appealing, but it creates a huge mess. Peter wrote about people who lead others into sin, saying these people "promise them freedom, but they themselves are slaves of corruption, since people are enslaved to whatever defeats them" (2 Pet. 2:19). They were slaves to their sin—it owned them, and they couldn't get out of it alone. Sometimes sin can look like freedom, but it's the opposite. Jesus is the only one who can and will bring freedom to our lives.

delight

What do you think it means to be free in Christ?

What are some examples of sins that seem promising or enticing? How do these sins ultimately lead to destruction?

How can you stand up against the sin that tempts you?

display

To defeat sin, you must be on your guard. Know the Word, let other people speak truth into your life, and rely on the Holy Spirit. If you don't have friends and trusted adults who will call you out on your sin, pray that God would bring these people your way. Pursue godly relationships that will point you back to Him.

Lord, help me stay free from the sins that tempt me. Give me the strength to stand up against them and run in the other direction. Help me to walk in the freedom that only You can give and to pursue the things you want me to pursue. Amen.

Fast and Slow

discover

READ 2 PETER 3:1-7.

They deliberately overlook this: By the word of God the heavens came into being long ago and the earth was brought about from water and through water.
— 2 Peter 3:5

Did you know that Netflix used to be a service that mailed DVDs to your house? If you were watching a series, you could only get a limited number of DVDs at a time and had to wait until you mailed one back to get the next one. Seriously, can you imagine waiting for the mail to deliver the next four episodes of your favorite show, rather than just pressing play on the next episode? Seems crazy, right?

The believers in Peter's day we were waiting. Peter explained to these believers that they may even see people questioning the second coming of Jesus. Two thousand years later, we're still waiting. There was and is a lot of waiting as a follower of Jesus.

While we wait, what do we know to be true? God's timing is perfect. We can never forget: He is the Creator of the world, and everything in it answers to Him. He will bring it to an end in His timing and according to His plan. We must live expectantly for that day, even if it occurs long after we're gone. God is the ultimate authority. It may feel like a long wait to us, but it isn't to God. Only He knows the timing. We don't know if it will be in our lifetime or not; we just have to trust Him. Thankfully, He has proven time and time again that He is trustworthy.

delight

Give an example of a time when you had to wait for longer than you wanted to. What was the situation? Were you patient or impatient? Why?

What did Peter remind the believers of in today's passage?

What does God want to teach you as you wait?

display

If you ask God to give you the opportunity to learn patience, He will. Be prepared to trust His timing, because He's never late. In the space below write about a time you experienced God's timing. How was His timing ultimately perfect? What did you learn as you waited?

God, help me to be patient and wait on You and Your best. Let me learn from Peter's reminders to trust You, no matter what. Amen.

Called to This

Time Travel

discover

READ 2 PETER 3:8-9.

**The Lord does not delay his promise, as some
understand delay, but is patient with you, not wanting
any to perish but all to come to repentance.
— 2 Peter 3:9**

Think back to the last time you traveled into a different time zone. How much of a difference did just one hour (or a couple of hours) make? Were you hungry and tired at all the wrong times? For us, just a little bit of time can make a huge difference. But God experiences time differently. Peter wrote that "with the Lord one day is like a thousand years, and a thousand years like one day" (2 Pet. 3:8). Can you even wrap your mind around that?

It's like God is in a totally different universe than we are. Oh, wait . . . He's God, and He's in charge of time! It's key to notice in this passage that Peter said God is patient with us. Can you believe it? God isn't just patient for the timing of what He wants; He is patient with each and every one of us. The Creator of the universe is willing to wait for those He loves.

Our minds are finite and so limited compared to His. He can see what we can't see, and He gives us every reason to trust Him. It is so important to remember that God desires for all to repent and come to faith in Him. He doesn't only love those who love Him back; He loves and desires to have a relationship with everyone in the world.

delight

Would you rather experience a day that's like a thousand years or a thousand years that are like a day? Why?

Have you ever experienced God's patience? What was that like?

Have you ever needed God to be patient with you? What was it like to know that the Lord of all was waiting on you?

display

Take a deep breath. Remind yourself that God is in control and that He loves you more than you can imagine. He can see what you're going through, and He knows your heart. Choose to trust Him today. Look back at page 85 of this devotion, and use it to memorize 2 Peter 3:9. Let this verse be a daily reminder of His love for you.

God, thank You for the hope that You always fulfill Your promises. Thank You that You are good and that You are patient with me. Help me to trust You with everything always. Amen.

Surprise Party

discover

READ 2 PETER 3:10-13.

Since all these things are to be dissolved in this way, it is clear what sort of people you should be in holy conduct and godliness.
— 2 Peter 3:11

Have you ever watched a movie in the theater and something jumped out suddenly? There's a really good chance that someone (surely, it wasn't you) screamed. Afterward, you probably thought, "I saw that coming." Well, Peter explains in this passage that absolutely no one will know the timing of Jesus's return. No one will see it coming.

There have been people throughout the history of the world who thought they knew when Jesus was coming back. So far, they've all been wrong. God's sovereignty, power, and timing are all bigger than we can grasp. When He says that He is the only one who knows, He means it. He's the only one who knows.

But no matter when the Lord returns, we should live our lives for Him and for His glory, seeking to obey and love Him while helping others come to know Him and do the same. Doing anything else would be a waste of our time. God has a new heaven and a new earth awaiting those who love and follow Him. It's going to be better than we could ever imagine!

When Jesus comes back, it will be the biggest, craziest surprise anyone has ever experienced. No one knows how to quite put it into words because we've never seen anything like it. Our job is to be prepared and share what we believe so as many others as possible are ready too.

delight

Who can you share Jesus with who doesn't know Him? How can you steer everyday conversations into spiritual conversations with this person?

What is the promise that Peter wrote about in verse 13? What does this promise mean for those who believe in Jesus?

display

Pray that God would show you some people in your life who don't yet know Him. Ask God for clear opportunities to share the gospel boldly with them. Take advantage of any opportunity you have to show them who Jesus is.

God, help me know how and when to share my faith. Don't let me miss an opportunity out of fear or pride. Let me share Your good news with courage. Amen.

Glory

discover

READ 2 PETER 3:14-18.

But grow in the grace and knowledge of our Lord and Savior Jesus Christ. To him be the glory both now and to the day of eternity.
— 2 Peter 3:18

Peter wrapped up this letter with words of encouragement to the believers of his day. His last challenge in verse 18 is to keep growing. We are on a faith journey. We will never arrive and be fully formed. We must continue to grow in our relationship with God throughout our entire life. He gets all of the glory for anything good in us, so we need to honor Him well with everything we say and do.

When we realize that our lives are about bringing glory to God, it changes everything. It's not about us at all; it's all about God. He is the hero of the story, and we are a part of that story, each doing our role. God is the Author, and He makes no mistakes. Our task of bringing glory to Him is the thing to which we must always return. He gets the glory now and in eternity.

Take advantage of every opportunity God gives you, and point all of it back to Him. We don't need to wait for spotlight moments like when we see actors and athletes thanking God at award ceremonies. It's in the day in, day out moments throughout our lives that He gets the glory. It's about giving Him the credit, even when no one else sees you doing it. Peter's challenge is for all of us today—don't miss it!

delight

Peter instructed his readers to grow in the grace and knowledge of Jesus. What are three ways you can continue to grow in this way?

How would your life change right now if you remembered every day that your life isn't about you at all?

display

Ask a friend to keep track of how often you talk about yourself over the course of a day or a week, and ask this friend to report back to you. What they have to say will probably surprise you, and you'll learn a lot from this experience. What if you interjected conversations about God instead of yourself? What could be different as a result?

God, let my life bring You glory in all that I say and do. I am Your servant and trust You with everything I am and have. Thank You for Your grace and salvation that You freely offer all of us. Amen.

THAT SOUNDS GOOD

It's often challenging to know when something is really from God's Word. Some phrases or ideas even get tossed around at church as truths from God that aren't actually from His Word at all. Let's test your ability to determine what's biblical and what just sounds good.

Write a T in the blank if you think the statement is biblical and an F in the blank if you think it isn't.

____ You are perfect the way you are.

____ You are enough/good enough.

____ God won't give you more than you can handle.

____ It's going to be okay.

____ This, too, will pass.

____ God helps those who help themselves.

____ As long as it makes you happy, go for it.

____ God will give me all the desires of my heart.

The line between truth and a lie can sometimes be razor thin—so much that there might be pieces of truth within the lie. Let's break these down.

You are perfect the way you are.

> **Read Romans 3:10.**

This idea is a misunderstanding or misquoting of Psalm 139:14. Yes, all people have intrinsic value given by God. All people are loved by God beyond what we can comprehend. However, only Jesus is perfect the way He is. Thankfully, when we trust in Him to save us and we give our lives to Him, He covers us with His righteousness. But this still doesn't mean we're perfect. We are constantly in a state of growth in righteousness as we mature in our relationship with God, and He promises to complete the good work He began in us (see Phil. 1:6). Yes, God loves you just the way you are. But He loves you too much to leave you that way.

You are enough/good enough.

Read Mark 10:18.

Mark 10:18 is Jesus's response to a man who called Him good and asked how to gain eternal life. Jesus explained that only God is good. Jesus is God, so Jesus is good. But we are not. God's standard is holy perfection, which we can never achieve on our own because we are born into sin (see Ps. 51:5). When we place our faith in Jesus, He gives us new life and brings us to fullness in Him (see Col. 2:9-10). We are not to be full of ourselves but to be filled with the Spirit, acknowledging that we will still mess up but understanding that God's grace is always enough.

God won't give you more than you can handle.

Read 1 Corinthians 10:13.

Jesus promises that we will suffer (see John 16:33). This is where we grow in our faith and learn to rely on God, who promises to help us stand up under the pressure the world puts on us. We could rephrase the statement above to accurately say, "God won't give you more than *He* can handle." We can be confident that whenever we are tempted, God will always provide a way out of the temptation so that we will not fall into sin. We just have to look for and take the way out that He provides.

It's going to be okay.

Read John 16:33.

As John 16:33 reminds us, we will have suffering in this world. However, our salvation is always secure in Jesus (see John 10:28-29). Ultimately, we can know that we will be okay because we know God keeps His promises. But we can't make guarantees about what life in the here and now will be like. What happens to us and what we go through is often *not* okay. Sometimes *we* are not okay. But we know God will never abandon us (see Matt. 28:20; Heb. 13:5) and that what lies ahead (that is, eternity with Him) is worth every broken piece of us (see Rom. 8:12). Even when tough days and tragedy and sadness come into our lives, God's goodness and love and our eternal security never change.

This, too, will pass.

Read 2 Corinthians 12:7.

This idea comes from a misreading of 1 Peter 5:10. Much like with "**It's going to be okay,**" the truth of this verse is that ultimately and eternally, God will restore us after we suffer. The hard part of that truth is that sometimes feelings in this life linger. Sometimes situations linger. Sometimes harmful people linger. Not everything "passes." Take Paul, for example. He had a "thorn in the flesh" after coming to know Christ, and as far as we know, God never took it away—despite Paul's prayers. We can count on facing tough things, but we can also count on God to walk with us through them.

God helps those who help themselves.

Read Ephesians 2:8-9.

Plenty of passages in the Bible praise hard work (see 2 Thess. 3:10-12; Prov. 12:24). God does call us to be diligent—but no amount of hard work can bring a person salvation. We can do nothing to earn God's grace. God doesn't want us to take matters into our own hands; He desires for us to wait on Him and be faithful to His Word. Jesus "helps" us by paying for our sin, offering us salvation, and sending the Holy Spirit. The Holy Spirit is called the Helper—the One who teaches us, strengthens us, gives us words to say, and even prays for us when we don't know what to pray. We don't have the kind of strength it takes to live God's way on our own—that's why He sent Jesus. We will never outgrow or outwork our need for Him.

As long as it makes you happy, go for it.

Read 1 Corinthians 10:23-24.

Our imperfect hearts sometimes lie to us (see Jer. 17:9), so their desires aren't always "good" or "right." This means that what makes us happy can't ever be good for us or others. Don't make the mistake of thinking God wants us to be rigid rule followers or unhappy people, either. Yes, God is holy and just, but we can't forget that God is also loving, gracious, and merciful. Scripture says God rejoices over His people and joy resounds in heaven when someone turns to follow Him (see Zeph. 3:17; Luke 15:7). Our good God loves to celebrate good things and give us good gifts (see Matt. 7:11; James 1:17). But Jesus said the most important commands are to love God and love others (see Matt. 22:36-40). We can't see how to love others well when we're only looking out for what makes us happy. Before you "go for it," ask yourself a few questions: Will it hurt me or someone else? Will it lead people to love God? What if this isn't going to tempt me to sin but it might tempt someone close to me to sin? God does want us to have joy—abundant, forever joy (see John 10:10)—but not at the expense of someone else's good.

God will give me all the desires of my heart.

Read Psalm 37:4 and Luke 11:9-13.

These verses dig into a misreading like we encountered with "**As long as it makes you happy, go for it**." When Jesus told His followers to ask, seek, and knock, He was teaching His followers to take everything to God in prayer. As we know, God is a good Father, and He wants to give us good gifts. This doesn't mean we'll get whatever we ask for or want—what we want and what's best for us aren't always the same. It means if we truly submit our desires to God, He changes our hearts over time to align with His will and purposes for us. Our changed hearts slowly begin to desire what God wants for us, and in this way, He gives us the desires of our hearts.

What other "almost" truths would you add to this list? What does Scripture really say about those statements?

Engage with God's Word.

lifeway.com/teendevotionals

☐ **THREE-IN-ONE**

☐ **IN THE BEGINNING**

☐ **TRUTH AND LOVE**

☐ **SEARCH AND KNOW**

☐ **TAKE UP AND FOLLOW**

☐ **THE SHEPHERD KING**

☐ **CHARACTER & COURAGE**

☐ **WORDS OF WISDOM**

☐ **PIONEER & PERFECTOR**

☐ **WITH YOU**

☐ **ROMANS**

☐ **LOVE AND JUSTICE**